GH00976221

VIVID BUILDING

VIVID BUILDING

drawings of the architecture of Ian Athfield and Roger Walker

Lewis E. Martin

The Dunmore Press

©1994 Lewis E. Martin
©1994 The Dunmore Press Limited

First Published in 1994
by
The Dunmore Press Limited
P.O. Box 5115
Palmerston North
New Zealand

ISBN 0 86469 213 7

Text: Nebraska 9.5/11
Printer: The Dunmore Printing Company Ltd, Palmerston North

Copyright. No part of this book may be reproduced without written permission except in the case of brief quotations
embodied in critical articles and reviews.

CONTENTS

Acknowledgements   6

Introduction   7

The 1960s   13

The 1970s   17

The 1980s and 1990   48

Index   102

About the Author   103

Dates refer to the dates of designing, not of completion.

ACKNOWLEDGEMENTS

The author wishes to thank the following, without whose encouragement and support this book would not have been published:

Resene Paints Ltd

New Zealand Lottery Grants Board

This is not a scholarly study. Rather, it is a celebration of the work of Athfield and Walker; it is an attempt on my part – a retired architect of a previous generation – to interpret and evaluate their work; it is an expression of my belief that they are more broadly significant than may generally be accepted; and it is a record which may help more people to understand and enjoy their buildings in particular, and New Zealand's buildings in general.

Some may wonder why I have made drawings rather than used photographs. I have enjoyed drawing buildings for over 40 years, but my own pleasure is no adequate explanation. It is said that the best way of finding out about something is to write a book about it. Drawing, like writing, absorbs time and energy and demands intense observation. I learn and understand more and more as I draw; when I have finished, it is as though I have consumed and digested the building, have experienced its essence and made it mine. And I am editing as I go – perhaps omitting trivialities, perhaps emphasising salient aspects. Consciously or unconsciously, a drawing becomes one person's interpretation and judgement upon another's work. This is perhaps the reason why people seem to respond more strongly to a drawing than to a photograph of a building; they discover fresh aspects which they do not otherwise appreciate. A drawing sometimes enables a fuller understanding than even the actual experience of the building.

In the same way, as I draw I learn more about the environment or context and about a building's relationship to it, and what I have learned is probably apparent in the completed drawing. It is only while working on the drawings that I have come to realise that Athfield and Walker are exceptionally sensitive to the environment.

Before I started this work, I might have thought Athfield and Walker sometimes merely amusing and clever; now I acknowledge the real significance of their work.

This book contains only a small selection of Athfield's and Walker's buildings. They each listed work which they had personally designed and wanted me to draw; so the primary selection is theirs. What I have finally drawn depended on the accessibility of the buildings, my own preferences, a need to include representative examples of each aspect of their work and my wish to demonstrate their range and diversity.

Commentaries on individual buildings are short – often no more than extended captions making one or two crucial points. I do not want to be adulatory; I want the drawings to speak for themselves and I have made no attempt to explain or describe in detail what is clearly visible. In any case, I find Athfield's and Walker's work largely inexplicable on a rational level. I can never give an answer to the question, 'Why did he do this?' To me, each building says, 'Here I am; accept me or reject me; interpret me as you will'.

Athfield and Walker must find it irritating to be bracketed as they often are. It seems unavoidable. Although their practices are quite separate, they arrived on the scene at about the same time; their early works were unprecedented and their designs over 25 years later are still easily distinguishable from those of their followers; some aspects of their early works had similarities, so that people were sometimes confused about the authorship; both are well-known nationally and their work has been published and described overseas; and both hold unconventional attitudes towards professional practice. But their designs are actually very different and it seems reasonable to conclude that their guiding principles also differ; certainly their work has evolved in divergent directions. However, I have chosen to bracket them in this book as I believe their influences have been crucial and have changed the direction of New Zealand architecture. In the notes which follow, I avoid comparisons and emphasise the qualities which both possess.

Athfield and Walker have fertile creative imaginations and are endlessly inventive. While often impossible to explain rationally, their works elicit deep responses at a subconscious or instinctive level. They are masters of lateral thinking and illuminating insight. Their works are robust and they have the courage to tackle the unfamiliar and to work without precedent.

It is common, but less so as time passes, for their buildings to be broken up into component parts. Walker has said that he sees a house as a microcosm of a city and that he wishes to make strong visual distinctions between various living spaces. The different portions are separately expressed and articulated.

Horizontal separation is compounded by variations in floor levels. Spaces are piled up vertically, often partly open to each other; staircases may open into living spaces at each half landing; accommodation may project out beyond or be recessed behind accommodation above or below. Vertically as well as horizontally, the component parts are separately identifiable.

Each discrete element is separately and straightforwardly designed to satisfy its particular needs; the resultant form is linked to its neighbours in what may appear to be an arbitrary fashion. Buildings assembled in this additive way are open-ended and easily capable of extension. We now accept all this easily, but the initial impact was often shocking; we were used to spaces contained within a more or less unified overall envelope.

Athfield and Walker share many well-recognised design elements, particularly in their early works – round windows, windows of unusual proportions, rooflights, exposed cross-braces, bottle-shaped and cylindrical towers, a profusion of nooks and crannies, soaring chimneys and flues, pipes as posts and as windows, rooflights and pinnacles. Varied window shapes combine in a dynamic balance; multiple floor levels and multiple verandahs relate to room needs and to the slopes of the land; glass is used in novel ways and with novel curves and shapes; plumbing pipes and other service elements – tanks, ventilators, ventilating trunking – do not hide away but become design elements and points of emphasis.

Few of their buildings do not startle; their vigorous innovations create endless interest. They can be whimsical and they have sometimes built jokes; they can be described in the same terms as Andy Warhol, of whom it has been said (by the Director of painting and sculpture in the Museum of Modern Art), 'He was a serious artist whose posture was unseriousness'.

What are the formative influences which, having been absorbed into their minds, have emerged afresh? New Zealand's colonial traditions are clearly important – verandahs, roof slopes and curves, dormers, finials, decoration, materials. Medieval and vernacular townscapes and roofscapes seem to be conscious influences, and Athfield's soft-edged white skins echo Mediterranean, Mexican and African traditions. There are hints of expressionism, Dutch Colonial and Art Deco; in fact there is probably little from the past that they have not absorbed and reminted as their own.

How can one discover any creative artist's intentions? Architects in particular are notoriously unable to analyse or articulate their own purposes; their writings and statements bewilder rather than clarify. We must form our own conclusions from the built evidence, or wait for time to pass and for historians to formulate theories.

If the term 'Post-Modernism' (as used of architecture) can be used to mean the modification of the puritanical International Style by enriching our buildings with well-known and well-loved motifs from the past, then Athfield and Walker were pioneering Post-Modernists. They have, however, little to do with the shallower forms of Post-Modernism, such as the application of simplified bits of the classical repertoire to otherwise impersonal surfaces.

Did they alone start a new wave, or were they the most visible figures in a generalised movement already under way? It may always be debated. They are certainly in the vanguard of a continuing architectural revolution in New Zealand. Many of the forms which they invented in their early works have become commonplace and their whole approach to design has encouraged a loosening up of attitudes and an increased respect for our own distinctive and vital traditions.

Nothing had prepared the architectural world for Athfield and Walker. They burst straight into the foreground, commanding attention with their outrageous novelties, bewildering the rest of us and compelling us to follow or admire or reject. Even before they had established their own practices, while they were still employed by others, they demonstrated their iconoclastic design imperatives with maturity and confidence. The Wellington Club, for example, designed by Walker as an employee, achieved fame and influence and became a rallying point before its demolition after some 20 years. Both men rapidly gained design responsibility within their employing firms and both seized their earliest opportunities to establish their own practices.

As is common for young architects, their early commissions were frequently for houses on precipitous or otherwise difficult sites. They produced such convincing and spectacular solutions that we suspected, at first, that these conditions were necessary to energise their powerful talents. Before long, however, they demonstrated an equal mastery in all circumstances.

Intending house owners, here and there, all over the country, have determined that, by hook or by crook, they would have an Athfield house or a Walker house, as the case may be. Architects are responsible for only a very small proportion of houses built, but it is probable that Athfield and Walker have increased the number of people wanting a house designed by a specific architect. Between them, they have by now designed some hundreds of houses and both have moved increasingly into other fields to become prolific, productive and successful.

They have developed and changed steadily and continually. Having had less time to absorb and accustom myself to their more recent works, I find these more difficult to evaluate and my comments on them may be seen to be the least assured.

Athfield and Walker have never been constrained by the normal limitations of professional practice. I do not mean that they have behaved unprofessionally; rather that they have always been prepared to provide services beyond those which are customary, starting by establishing closer than normal relations with their clients. In their early days, many people who wanted their houses lacked the resources to follow the normal patterns of construction. Then – and it is still true today – many owners did much of their own building, helped and supported by the architects who became valued friends. They have always avoided any sense of the architect being remote, dignified and pontifical.

I have met owners, occupiers and users of many of their buildings; nearly all have expressed their continuing delight and pride. Purchasers of Athfield's and Walker's houses previously built for others have been at pains to consider and consult the original architect before making extensions and alterations. Unusual attention seems to have been paid to gardening, landscaping and the preservation of the natural environment; these are worked out to complement the buildings, to enhance them and to be, in their turn, enhanced by them. Inside and out, occupiers give loving care and attention to the use of the buildings and to their surroundings. Since I drew it, one of the houses has been burned to the ground, and has been rebuilt in almost exactly the same form.

Athfield's and Walker's work is still steadily evolving; no summation can yet be made. All that can be said is that they are pioneers who have produced architecture which is unique by any standards in the world. I like to think that they are in the vanguard of a creative wave originating in the Pacific basin.

House, Highbury, Wellington

This, the first house that Roger Walker designed after graduation, already demonstrates his mastery of vertical space – volumes open to one another above and below, with light filtering downwards as well as entering horizontally. The unusual room arrangements needed to achieve these qualities determine the external forms and give them Walker's characteristic flavour – upward expansion, powerful separate roof shapes, and seemingly random windows in walls and roofs.

Two Houses, Khandallah, Wellington

The nearest house, full of sweeping roof curves, is piled up high to grasp the view and accommodate the fall in the land. Beyond and to the left is Athfield's own ever-expanding and ever-surprising house, set on a spur commanding the harbour, topped by the lookout which has become a Wellington landmark.

House, Seatoun Heights, Wellington

The owners struggled unsuccessfully for months to plan the house they wanted on their small steep section overlooking the sea. When they finally turned to Athfield, he gave them the traditional room arrangement and the many outdoor living areas they sought, all within their budget. They describe it as warm, flowing, practical, original and designed for enjoyment. The dramatic white and black shapes flow down the undisturbed landscape of coastal bush with a seeming inevitability.

House, Wilton, Wellington

The slope is precipitous – the entrance from the road is above the highest point seen here. Land, vegetation and house are inextricably interlocked. Glimpses can be had but no complete view of the house is possible.

House, Highbury, Wellington

At the age of ten Roger Walker built 'Fort Nyte' – a four-storied tower of waste timber in the back yard. Here is one of its earliest lineal descendants. A series of timber and glass towers and galleries stands on a robust masonry base, whose windows are supplemented by vertical pipes, one pair of which pass right through an upper gallery.

The varied shapes, stepping up the slope like separate buildings, form an intensely complex and yet coherent whole.

House, Khandallah, Wellington

The site is on an exposed windswept hilltop, closely locked in by other houses. Shelter and privacy have been gained by building connected pavilions around a garden court. Square red finials top the wigwam-like blocks rising from rocks and vegetation.

House, Korokoro, Petone

Given the opportunity of a large semi-rural site, Walker spreads this house out and down in relaxed fashion in its luxuriant setting of garden and trees. The miniature room perched up high catches a harbour view through trees and hills.

City Council Housing – Arlington Stage I, Wellington

The intricately-related low-rise townhouses are dense with visual interest – varying heights, roof slopes and roof lines; windows sized and placed irregularly as required; plumbing pipes exposed as decorative elements; steps and stairs; sunken courts, gardens, yards, twisting alleyways, play areas, concrete block and timber walls and screens.

The main body of the block of flats, on the other hand, has a calm regularity and a gently syncopated rhythm of windows and bands; until it suddenly explodes, at the top and one end, into a whole village of shapes.

Eight Townhouses, Wellington

This riot of forms, finished overall in white, terminates a
steep street. Seen from the town below, with a background
of dark evergreens, it might be a temple sculptured in ice.
Each house is distinctive; the stepping forms give multiple
private north-facing terraces or verandahs and views to the
west over the centre of Wellington.

Centrepoint, Masterton

Sixteen shops of various sizes and shapes, each having its own distinctive form, are disposed around an internal top-lit brick-paved courtyard, emulating the atmosphere of open-air markets. The observation tower dominates and gives the town a central landmark.

St. Columban's Mission, Lower Hutt

This is the mission's central house for New Zealand and Australia; missionaries, mostly working in the southern hemisphere, return here for rest periods and retirement. The limited range of simple materials is spartan and monastic; but the complex forms and the verandahs give a homelike character. Interiors are enriched by precious belongings and mementoes brought from exotic places of work.

Whakatane Airport

A brilliant theatrical introduction to a provincial town. The stylistic characteristics – round windows, pipes, cross-braces, rooflights and cylindrical towers – create a matrix which comfortably absorbs the technical gadgetry of public address outlets, aerials, meteorological equipment, telephones, lights, air-conditioners, signboards, etc. It all establishes exactly the right mechanistic quality. In a deft touch, a stairway runs up the slope of the roof to emphasise the pyramidal form.

Park Mews, Wellington

Confronted by the almost baffling complexity of the group as a whole, it is difficult to believe that, in fact, most of the thirty apartments have a similar basic plan. Variety is achieved by different orientation, random grouping and varied roofs, balconies, sundecks, windows and fireplaces. Some minor alterations and additions have been made in the years since construction, and one, at least, is clearly not designed by the architect. But all demonstrate how the irregular shapes accommodate or even encourage modifications to suit individual occupants. (It is a pity that the whole site could not be obtained; the incompatible low units intrude.)

House, Seatoun Heights, Wellington

The house climbs a very steep hill above the sea like a village on eight levels, throwing up a spectacular series of turrets, pinnacles, and glazed eyries as it goes. Save from a helicopter, it is nearly impossible to gain an overall view. Rooms open to paths and gardens on many levels and here, in the centre, there is a well-used, sheltered, sunny living court overlooking sea and hills.

House, Glenfield, Auckland

A delicious back yard; wigwams pierced with glass; blocks stepped down the slopes; characteristically Walker, but subtly modulated so as to be also characteristically Auckland.

House, Eastbourne

Only a few metres from the sea, this house squeezes in between the road and a cliff covered in coastal scrub and bush. The structure and the shapes are sheer bravura, spreading out from twin unequal bottle-shaped towers of second-hand bricks. One tower contains the staircase; alternate landings give access one way or the other, serving floor levels half a storey apart. Unadorned timber poles, braces, struts and beams carry rooms wherever space allows and a verandah like a platform in a tree.

House, Mahina Bay, Wellington

In idiom, this is a lineal descendant of colonial cottages; but its complexity of forms and roof slopes owes nothing to tradition. Once again, the house is so completely at home on its cliff above the sea that it might almost be a natural form.

RNZEME Workshops, Waiouru Military Camp

Strictly rational metalwork, sharp and trim, refined
in detail and handled with flair.

House, New Plymouth

Many will find this readily recognisable as Walker's; some will count it as a 'Noddy House' – a derisive term applied indiscriminately to the work of Walker and Athfield lumped together. It is, in fact, no more representative of Walker's work than any other of his widely varied buildings in this book. It is one more distinctive expression of fertile and imaginative creativity.

House, Horokiwi, Wellington

The architect as sculptor; the all-enveloping white
skin encourages the moulding of shapes, most notably
the remarkable chimneys. Set on green hills and
against a background of bush, the arresting image
of the house is visible for miles.

House, Seatoun, Wellington

Many characteristic elements are here – emphatic chimney and pipes; a dynamic balance of unusually shaped windows; multiple floor levels; and verandahs opening to various aspects of slope, views and sun. But the house as a whole is uncharacteristically calm and unspectacular under its broad restful expanses of roof.

Farmhouse, Opaki

Materials – poles, brick, shingles and unpainted weatherboards – are close to nature; shapes are relaxed and sprawling; brick walls enclose gardens and orchards and extend the building outwards into the park-like farmland; the vast fireplace forms the centre of a window wall; its extraordinary spire of a chimney creates a vertical punctuation mark in scale with the macrocarpas. The house is completely at home in the Wairarapa plain.

House, Castor Bay, Auckland

Tucked away in a bush-filled valley, this house makes
no grand statement, but revels in its compact diversity,
turning inwards upon its intimate and varied open
spaces.

Greta Point Tavern, Wellington

Old shipping company stores have been converted
into a tavern and restaurant. Internally, trusses,
oregon linings and jarrah floors are retained. The
roof is reshaped, and the dark corrugated iron
exterior is enlivened by roof vents, verandah posts
with triangular steel brackets, and a wall of windows
opening the tavern to the whole bay.

Cable Car Halts, Wellington

Informal and casual shelters with Victorian overtones blend
with the engineering works and contrast with the car itself.
Games are played with the special elements – platforms,
stairs, ramps, overbridges, balustrades and handrails;
robustly constructed in traditional timber and steel, they
make radical and exciting forms.

House, Okuku

Pavilions radiate at various angles from the central core; giant pipes accommodate bed spaces; roof lines are alive with prickles, pipes and finials. The forms, typical of Walker's work, stand out especially sharply in the plains of Canterbury.

Willis Street Village, Wellington

The village of shops, cafes and restaurants is picturesque, flamboyant and possibly evanescent. Its playful roof forms contrast totally with the Dixon Street government flats, one of our first, largest and finest buildings in the puritanical early International Style.

Winemaker's House, Havelock North

The winemaker wanted to live in the midst of his vines, to know them as he knows his family. One verandah is quite open to them; another outdoor living-space is more secluded and a little ceremonial.

The soft flowing shapes within the all-enveloping white skin are reminiscent of idealised African villages; they meld into a dynamic balance and unity. The house meanders up and down, to and fro, responding to the needs of the several rooms and the slope of the gentle valley.

Rocklands Farmhouse, Clifton, Takaka

Echoing the forms of old farm buildings, the house spreads itself on a knoll, backed by looming hills, commanding Golden Bay. Above eaves level, it reflects the power of the scarps, revelling in strong contrasting textures: rock chimneys; corrugated iron; and rough unpainted timber shingles capped at ridges and hips with shaped tree trunks. Below the eaves, its gentle flowing lines and harmonious materials grow out of and relate to the knoll.

50

House, Governors Bay, Lyttelton Harbour

The crisp white shapes top an isolated hill; from each direction the components group up into a fresh image.

Elements not normally treated as significant parts of a building have become dominant features. The design originally included twin tanks at the apex; reducing them to one has been a regrettable change.

House, Dalefield, near Queenstown

Alterations to a cottage in a luxuriant hollow in the huge glaciated landscape.

This and the three widely varied country houses which precede it were all designed in the same year.

On the one hand, they show common characteristics of Athfield's work at this time – low sprawling assemblies of varied shapes with powerful vertical accents. On the other, they demonstrate his extreme flexibility, his readiness to match his work to the character and wishes of his clients and, above all else, his acute sense of the genius of the place and of the building appropriate to it.

Entrance to Waitomo Caves

Mature trees hide an informal scatter of strong shapes clad
in casual rustic brick and shingles. Paving ties all together
and curves up into low walls and seats; cabbage trees and
windmill imitate one another; public toilets are transmuted
into emblematic roadside roundhouses.

First Church of Christ Scientist, Wellington

The congregation wanted a building open to the street, presenting a memorable image, and without traditional religious symbolism. The entrance is at the junction of low and high parts with auditorium to left and meeting rooms to right. The extraordinarily organic shape encloses the organ loft, lit by an eye of stained glass. Is the cranked column a joke? Whatever its meaning, it is completely right in its context.

The Shamrock, Wellington

An old city hotel has been preserved by being moved, altered, extended and converted into specialist shops and restaurant. In its original form, the building was a simple L-shape; Athfield has provided verandahs, staircases, low extensions and additional work to the adjoining house; all demonstrate his respect for and sympathy with nineteenth century work.

James Cook Arcade, Wellington

This small office building and shopping arcade (leading to lifts serving a hotel and car-parking building above and behind) is quite astonishing in its use of colour and exposed tapering ducts and in the shapes of roofs, arcade and verandah. It captures all the excitement inherent in a spectacular part of the city, where buildings are backed up against tall blocks on the Terrace about ten stories higher up.

House overlooking Hamilton Lake

The lawn runs right from the lake edge up the living room; climbing plants give summer privacy from boats.

Vertical pipes, spikes and finials run riot and bargeboards are fretted into cascades of drooping stalactites – 'high colonial excitement' in Walker's words.

Stock and Station Agency, Tapanui

This is the scene as one enters Tapanui from the south, a splendid introduction to a small town. Simple colonial forms and materials, carefully planted and nurtured, recreate an extended and idealised traditional country general store.

Western Park Tavern, Wellington

The renovation of an old hotel, which had been altered so often that the possibility of authentic restoration no longer existed. Corrugated iron, once disreputable, becomes a sharply sophisticated skin with its horizontal lines, rounded corners and graphics of extreme elegance. The concept – a conservatory elevated on attenuated steel columns and attached to a sleek shed – is elementary, and yet it creates a distinctive and appropriate image.

House, Havelock North

The owners' previous house on the site had been destroyed by fire, leaving only the swimming pool. This, together with the superb views and the mature garden, conditioned planning decisions.

There are several normally disparate flavours: the nautical – fine polished stainless steel posts, rails, flues, struts and stays, the external stairway and the precise white 'flying bridge'; the mediterranean – soft-edged flowing stucco surfaces, most prominent on the entrance side; the gallic – segmental-headed shuttered windows; and the indigenous – relaxed verandahs and sun-porches.

I find this house absolutely beautiful, absolutely spectacular and absolutely livable.

House, Lake Wakatipu

Unfinished though it is, something exciting is clearly happening here. Against the over-bearing hill and craggy landscape, the sturdy house has the flavour of old buildings in the mountainous centre of France; but there are light-hearted elements too: a barbecue court is hollowed out of an otherwise stern rectangle; and the rocks which retain terraces extend up gable end walls, petering out between and alongside windows.

Melrose Lodge, Whitford

Overlooking the verdant countryside between suburban Auckland and the Hunua ranges, this is both farmhouse and exclusive guesthouse, complete with self-contained flat, luxurious guest bedrooms, billiard room, pool, spa pool and helicopter hangar. Even more than most Athfield houses, it displays different characters in different parts, ranging all the way from a garden front with columns and shuttered french doors to a courtyard of traditional colonial shapes.

Staff Housing, Chateau Tongariro

The small group is set back against a grove of beech trees; individual units face out, each with its own semi-enclosed open space. Front doors all open from this sheltered courtyard, decorated with alpine plants and made cheerful by the playful parapets, window shapes, individual porch roofs, lights and supergraphics.

Palmerston Road, Gisborne

Built as workshop and showroom for a plumber and
metalworker, this striking structure demonstrates and
extends the possible ways of using metals. The quarter
circles created by the cascading roof are couterpointed
by quarter-circular glazing, semi-circular brickwork and
an ebullient fantasy of semi-circular tubular ventilators.

Cable-car Terminal and Cables Restaurant, Wellington

The relaxed atmosphere of the adjoining Botanical Gardens continues in the rambling building shapes and the trelliswork. A conservatory serves as a bus shelter and links the cable-car terminus to the restaurant. Service elements are important in the design: some are visible punctuation marks on the roof; others are encased within louvres and trellised domes which make interplays of lines and transparencies with the glass roofs and walls. The restaurant trelliswork extends down to frame an entrance like a grotesque face.

Energy Direct Building, Lower Hutt

Here is an office block as full of life and vigour as most are full of tedium.

Office windows are well-shaded by precast concrete eyelids; entrance and flanking spaces are sheltered by aerial conservatories; pavilions appear at various levels with sloping roofs and glass-topped verandahs; fire-escape stairways cascade to and fro to the ground; a glass curtain wall turns into an emblematic mural; and the mast-spire is appropriately high-tech.

Townhouses, Ngaio, Wellington

Five townhouses of varying size have been shoe-horned into a suburban section, but there is no sense of crowding. A courtyard to the south gives car and foot access; houses look outwards into garden courts or northwards over a small reserve. The formal language is based on single-slope roofs, often coming to an apex on a corner.

House, Barrytown, near Punakaiki

Although it is difficult to define why, the house is
unmistakably of the West Coast. It perches on a shelf
on a typical hill of bush regenerating through gorse,
spread open to the Tasman and the sunsets. Not quite
complete, it is being lovingly finished by its owners.

House, Roseneath, Wellington

There are two dwellings on this precipitous site. One is topped by the semi-circular vault; the other, the main house, is spread round a high-level courtyard behind the glass passage above the arched main entrance.

The building is an exercise in curves, stairs and diagonals, carried out in brick, white or colour-washed plaster, beautiful creamy ashlar stonework and fine metalwork. But what are we to make of the bizarre stone columns twisted into spirals?

Hewlett Packard Building, Wellington

The building establishes a powerful image of extreme sleek refinement; smooth frameless black glass is precisely flush with glossy white tiled walls; both flow smoothly round the tower; metalwork glitters in balustrades, conservatory framing, gutter, lettering, spherical column tops and column 'spats'.

The conservatory-verandah-gallery over the footpath is a wonderful space (open to two floor levels) for conferring, relaxing, or just for watching the world go by.

Courtyard Roof, Victoria University of Wellington

A transparent roof of metal, glass and plastic sheeting has been built over a central court of irregular shape and level, surrounded by disparate buildings. At first sight it merely dazzles, but gradually the form becomes clear. Another designer might have imposed a large simple shape with a regular pattern; but Athfield has typically dealt with each formal problem separately and straightforwardly, achieving richness through diversity.

Wairakei Resort Hotel – Spa Pools

Glass-roofed spaces, reminiscent of wigwams, shelter
behind walls of ponga logs.

Wairakei Resort Hotel – Laundry

Extraordinarily cheerful, playful and inventive for
so workaday a purpose.

Wairakei Resort Hotel – Playstructure

Play elements – slide, steps, stairs, ladders, flying fox
and swings – are intricately interwoven within a
framework that carries the rainbow and the 'possum
and weka weathervanes.

Beach House, Omaha

Set in the middle of a huge new seaside development, this house is really quite simple and straightforward; an L-shaped plan opens all rooms on to a secluded, sunny court on the ocean side. But on the landward, street side, what a statement is made! It partly rejects and partly satirises the ubiquitous brown-stained-and-white-painted kitsch. Black walls topped by false parapets are extended by shaped black trellises; curved canopies burst out in boiled-sweet colours; and tanks (elsewhere concealed as if embarrassing) are flaunted.

House, Ngaio, Wellington

An exercise in diagonals, triangles and 'prickles', set off by the round tower, the twin flues and the arched beam to the garage. Roofs are covered in metal sheeting, and so are most exterior walls apart from the windows and the brickwork.

House, Karehana Bay, Plimmerton

Here is a more formal, less casual, expression of Walker's characteristic concepts. There are fewer elements; the interplay of contrasting one-way-sloped roofs is rigorously controlled; but there are new games with windows curving through 90°, 135° and even 225°.

Renovated Commercial Building, Wellington

The original building, of the late '20s, met all the demands of its important corner situation but had become shabby and unattractive. In his thorough-going refurbishment, Athfield has concentrated external alterations and additions at the edges; so the original central bulk is enriched at top, bottom and ends. The new neo-classical elements – columns, balconies, gables, parapets and cornices – have a Dutch Colonial flavour.

Former DFC Treasury, Wellington

A merchant bank established itself in an upper floor of the old DIC Building – once a department store.

Working hours were long and concentrated. Staff found contrast and relief in a boulevard which ran the full length, ending in glass doors opening on to a verandah overlooking Lambton Quay. Officers met, rested and conferred on park benches. Working areas, dealers' rooms and mezzanines flanked the boulevard. The setting is magical, flooded with light, glittering with silver trees, white paint, tiles and marble, glass blocks and polished stainless steel.

Taranaki Service Station, Stratford

Four glass umbrellas shelter the forecourt, each carried on a central pole above a brick cylinder. The slopes of the glass carry on down to a low level at front and back, but not at the ends so there is ample clearance for tall vehicles. The working area is light and bright and unusually well-sheltered.

The owners express satisfaction and pride; they maintain the buildings and garden carefully and keep it all splendidly free of clutter.

Resort Hotel, Queenstown

An unusually formal and symmetrical design gives a court with a sense of luxurious sun-drenched seclusion in the middle of this feverish tourist town. Aluminium grillages make points of emphasis and add sparkle to the crisp white walls topped with shaped parapets and pyramidal towers.

House, Maungaraki, Lower Hutt

The various parts of the house are separately identified in strikingly different shapes. The mechanistic round-topped parts contrast especially sharply with the cottagy weatherboarded sections, which are full of traditional elements and forms.

Walker and Athfield often establish unusually close relationships with the owners of the houses they design; owners are often unusually deeply involved in the establishment of their place to live; and, as here, they often complete the building and finishing work themselves.

Centre City, New Plymouth

No single viewpoint can capture the totality of this vast complex, which covers three city blocks. It accommodates a department store, a supermarket, 55 shops and 750 cars, all accessible from a glass-vaulted atrium. The bulk has been broken down into separate elements enriched with sloping columns carrying beams as it were on brackets, with semi-circular parapet shapes and with machine rooms spreading out as they rise.

Externally, the appearance of the atrium belies its size; internally, it is a majestic space, within which the dynamic fluid lines of mammoth ventilating trunks counterpoint the powerful axial symmetry of the escalators.

Telecom House, Wellington

The side of the building follows the lane which is not perpendicular to the street; so the street face is broken into a series of steps which add interest and reduce the effect of mass.

In the upper stories, the bones of the structure are hidden behind a sleek skin of glass and smooth tiles, softened by curved corners. In the lower stories, however, the structure is exposed with giant three-storey-high columns and a two-storied stepped verandah canopy of flexible translucent material.

Beyond the main tower, at a low level, are five apartments; three are visible from the street.

The facade glows in early morning light reflected from the glass walls of nearby buildings.

Luxury Apartments, Oriental Bay, Wellington

In most of the dwellings which he has designed, Athfield has had very close contact with those who occupy them. Quite different conditions apply here – the design has had to be impersonal, related only to the environment.

The Oriental Bay environment is exceptional – luxury accommodation on expensive land looking out on to the harbour across a lively urban marine playground.

The block dramatises its situation with crashing contrasts between solid side walls and the possibly impractical all-glass front; it is highly sophisticated; and there is perhaps an element of satire – echoes of the formalised oriental opulence of Hollywood epics of the 1930s.

House, Havelock North

Built for a poet and a potter, this house is so embowered in an old garden that it can never be seen completely. Although it appears simple and modest, it contains many spaces at varied levels, almost all of which are furnished with their own individual livable verandahs.

Ropata Village, Lower Hutt

To the left are pensioners' flats and communal spaces; to the right and out of the picture, along the main road, is a medical centre. The complex cubist and curving forms provide verandahs for all flats, some open, some screened against noise where appropriate. In addition to its sculpted profile, the skyline is decorated with vestigial bits of wooden structures (Walker's 'fragments of memory').

Indian Sports and Cultural Centre, Kilbirnie, Wellington

A factory has been adapted to a surprisingly different use.

Athfield, always ready to fall in with his clients' wishes, has achieved a powerful effect by the simple device of creating a grand portico and surrounding the low block by a freestanding arcade, all in simplified traditional Indian forms.

Library, Wellington

This building, one of the new structures surrounding the new civic square, has two contrasting faces. On the sunny street side, it presents civic grandeur – urbane solid walls, recessed arcade, monumental but inviting entrance; all enhanced by columns in the form of nikau palms. On the other side, the south-eastern face of the library is completely opened to the civic square with a four-storey-high serpentine glass wall, which includes another prominent entrance at mezzanine level.

Inside, a visitor is immediately aware of all the library and its component parts; the overwhelming impression is one of transparency, airiness and spaciousness. Along the great curving window wall are secluded reading and lounging areas at every level, looking on to ponds and the civic square but untroubled by sun. The two entrances are connected through mezzanine exhibition areas (with meeting rooms) and a lively cafe; the library is in full view but security is not compromised.

All the librarians' hopes and requirements have been met. In the first year of operation, borrowings have increased by up to 50% and visits by 90%.

Provincial Centre for the Marist Order, Wellington

A sunny, secluded corner in the extensive development.
Its light-hearted, informal and human quality contrasts
sharply with its aloof and disapproving neighbour.

House, Eastbourne

Walker's romanticism is well to the fore here. The luxurious and livable house snuggles back into the steep tree-filled valley. Separate wings hinge about the circular stair towers; one staircase spirals round a circular chimney which carries flues from two fireplaces below. What shapes could better complement this rich environment?

INDEX

A
airport 26
alterations and renovations 43, 53, 57, 60, 74, 84, 85, 96
apartments 20, 28, 29, 92, 93, 95
Arlington 20
Auckland 31, 42, 65

B
Barrytown 72
Bay of Plenty 26
beach house 79

C
cable car 44, 45, 68
Canterbury 46, 51
Castor Bay 42
Centre City 90, 91
Centrepoint 24
Chateau Tongariro staff housing 66
Church of Christ Scientist 56
City Council housing 20
civic square 99
Clifton 50
courtyard roof, VUW 74

D
Dalefield 53
department store 90, 91
DFC Treasury, former 85
DIC building 85
Dixon St flats 47

E
Eastbourne 33, 101
Energy Direct Building 69

F
farmhouses 36, 40, 41, 46, 50, 64, 65
flats 20, 28, 29, 47, 92, 93, 95

G
general store 61
Gisborne 67
Glenfield 31
Golden Bay 50
Governors Bay 51
Greta Point Tavern 43

guest-house 65

H
Hamilton Lake 59
Havelock North 48, 62, 63, 94
Hawke's Bay 48, 62, 63, 94
Hewlett Packard Building 75
Highbury 13, 16
Horokiwi 36
houses 13, 14, 15, 16, 17, 18, 19, 22, 23, 30, 31, 32, 33, 35, 36, 39, 40, 41, 42, 46, 48, 50, 51, 53, 59,62, 63, 64, 65, 70, 72, 73, 79, 81, 82, 88, 94, 101
housing 20, 66
Hunua Ranges 65

I
Indian Sports and Cultural Centre 96
Interact 87
interiors 74, 85, 91, 99

J
James Cook Arcade 58

K
Karehana Bay 82
Khandallah 14, 19
Kilbirnie 96
King and Dawson 20
King Country 54, 55
Korokoro 18

L
Lake Wakatipu 64
laundry 77
library 98, 99
Lower Hutt 25, 69, 88, 95
luxury apartments 93
Lyttelton Harbour 51

M
Mahina Bay 32
Marist Order 100
Masterton 24
Maungaraki 88
medical centre 95
Melrose Lodge 65
merchant bank 85

military camp 34
mission 25

N
New Plymouth 35, 90, 91
Ngaio 70, 81
Nightingale, Inkster and Bentall 69
Northland 79

O
offices, office buildings 58, 69, 75, 84, 85, 92
Okuku 46
Omaha 79
Opaki 40, 41
Oriental Bay 93
Otago 53, 61, 64, 87

P
Park Mews 28, 29
pensioners' flats 95
Petone 18
play structure 78
Plimmerton 82
Poverty Bay 67
Provincial Centre for the Marist Order 100
public toilets 55
Punakaiki 72

Q
Queenstown 53, 64, 87

R
renovations and alterations 43, 53, 57, 60, 74, 84, 85, 96
resort hotel 76, 77, 78, 87
restaurant 43, 47, 57, 68
RNZEME workshops 34
Rocklands 50
Ropata Village 95
Roseneath 73

S
St Columban's Mission 25
Seatoun 15, 30, 39
service station 86
Shamrock, the 57
shopping centre 90, 91

shops 24, 47, 57, 58, 61, 91
showroom 67
spa pools 76
sports and cultural centre 96
staff housing, Chateau Tongariro 66
stock and station agency 61
Stratford 86
supermarket 90, 91

T
Takaka 50
Tapanui 61
Taranaki 35, 86, 90, 91
Taranaki Service Station 86
taverns 43, 60
Telecom House 92
tourist hotels 76, 77, 78, 87
townhouses 20, 22, 23, 70

U
university 74

V
Victoria University of Wellington 74
visitor centre 54, 55
Volcanic Plateau 34, 66, 76, 77, 78

W
Waikato 59
Waiouru Military Camp 34
Wairakei Resort Hotel 76, 77, 78
Waitomo Caves 54, 55
Wairarapa 24, 40, 41
Wakatipu, Lake 64
Watt, Gus 58
Wellington 13, 14, 15, 16, 17, 19, 20, 22, 23, 28, 29, 30, 32, 36, 39, 43, 44, 45, 47, 56, 57, 58, 60, 68, 70, 73, 74, 75, 81, 84, 85, 92, 93, 96, 98, 99, 100
West Coast 72
Western Park Tavern 60
Whakatane 26
Whitford 65
Willis Street Village 47
Wilton 17
winemaker's house 48
workshops 34, 67

Lewis Martin was born and grew up in Napier. He studied architecture in Auckland and, after war years in the Fleet Air Arm, stayed on in London, studying and working there for eight years. On returning home, he practised in Wellington until retirement. He has always drawn buildings; a 1948 travelling scholarship to Spain resulted in a report consisting solely of drawings. He has had one previous book published in 1987 – *Points of View* – in praise of the New Zealand built environment.